The Way the Moon

Holly Haworth's *The Way the Moon* shares its being with the moon itself, and the poems know what the moon knows: that the light we shine is never ours alone. Each new line break, breath, and page takes me further into the truth that even the smallest of us, and the most hurting, carry the whole Earth within. Or, as the poet writes, "Love is not born once but must / give birth to itself again & again." This astonishing debut lives in my heart next to Louise Glück's *The Wild Iris* and CD Wright's *Casting Deep Shade*. Haworth has given us transformation, a true work of art.

—Rebecca Gayle Howell, author of *Render /
An Apocalypse* and *American Purgatory*

Haworth's collection is a gorgeous recital of "clear-throated singing," a hymn to and for a creation that has not yet (despite humankind's best intentions) been divested of the numinous. What does one do when a place becomes "everything I needed?" One needs more, and better; differently, and in present tense. The sumptuous poems record the fulfillment and enlargement of a desire that is both satiated by and reflected urgently in the observed world, the all that is not-I, the not-self. Their opulence gleams and rings in the "cast-iron night."

—G.C. Waldrep, author of *The Earliest Witnesses*

In Holly Haworth's debut book of poems, *The Way the Moon*, the speaker whispers, "I am abandoned   to the land." And this quiet abandonment allows multitudes of beings of the Blue Ridge Mountains to shimmer and speak. I trust Haworth's earned bodily intimacy, with her "basketsful of nettle/ armsful of fennel," the lived knowing, the sorrowful and ecstatic inside these poems. I want to read these lyric spells by candlelight, by moonlight—slip from human habit and disperse into this enchanted, tangled wild place.

—Anne Haven McDonnell, author of *Breath on a Coal* and recipient
of a 2023 NEA Literature Fellowship in Creative Writing

The Way the Moon spellbinds. The poems yearn. And yodel. The poems see. And pine. Together we wander with Haworth over her homeland loams. Somewhere Dorothy Wordsworth keeps time with an apple-switch while Dock Boggs sings like a coyote full of rabbit and rain. Haworth gifts us nothing short of the sublime. I had to sit while reading these poems because they floored me. I had to stand and do a little dance because Haworth's music would not let my knees keep still. Such is the fecund gambol you are in for, Dear Reader. And I have a mind to plant each and all of her heirloom words. And I'll be hoping for a rhubarb the size of a cathedral. Let's all meet there soon. Next full moon.

—Abraham Smith, author of *Insomniac Sentinel* and *Dear Weirdo*

The Way the Moon

Poems

HOLLY HAWORTH

MERCER UNIVERSITY PRESS
MACON, GEORGIA

MUP/ P708

28 27 26 25 24   5 4 3 2 1

Books published by Mercer University Press are printed on acid-free paper that meets the
requirements of the American National Standard for Information Sciences—Permanence of
Paper for Printed Library Materials.

Printed and bound in the United States.

This book is set in Garamond.

Cover design by Burt&Burt.

ISBN   978-0-88146-944-8
Library of Congress Cataloging-in-Publication Data

Names: Haworth, Holly, author.
Title: The way the moon : poems / Holly Haworth.
Description: Macon, Georgia : Mercer University Press, 2024. |
Identifiers: LCCN 2024020026 | ISBN 9780881469448 (paperback; acid-free
   paper)
Subjects: LCGFT: Poetry.
Classification: LCC PS3608.A8948 W39 2024 | DDC 811/.6--dc23/eng/20240508
LC record available at https://lccn.loc.gov/2024020026

For the ancestors of Floyd County

He used to hear the voice of Artemis
Calling out to him in the lunar
No man's land of the mountains

    Alice Oswald

Barn's burnt down—
now I can see the moon.

    Mizuta Masahide,
      Trans. Lucien Stryk and Takashi Ikemoto

These poems were written over the course of a year in the Blue Ridge Mountains with each of the moon's thirteen cycles. Each poem was written in four phases: from new moon to first quarter, first quarter to full, full to last quarter, and last quarter to new.

MERCER UNIVERSITY PRESS

Endowed by

TOM WATSON BROWN
and
THE WATSON-BROWN FOUNDATION, INC.

Contents

Magnolia

1

>   —& the moon flowers out
>   of the dusk

a whisp, one white petal.

>   A chipped tooth in time's maw & cruel jaws

above the bent horizon of mountains.

>   You were a child once
>   & once the earth was young.

I record the changes of the seasons
>   for years
to come. What years
>   will come, the seasons rearranged—what strange-
ness. I am dumb. I ink
>   dark nectar leaked
down from the tongue,
>   this almanac.

>   The breath before & after

>   a flower opens, the air

around it torn to perfumed shreds.

The lungs' six hundred

>   million alveoli
>   are an inflorescence breast-hidden,

the voice blooming up.

The laced blood of the moon.

A seed that precedes
or follows
language.

In the atmosphere
a current, quest-
ion.

2

My throat a cumulus.

The moon looms the limbs of cedars.

The air it is honeysuckled. Fields clovered
                              since the Cretaceous.

After a thunderstorm
rolls past Purgatory Mountain,
    I harvest from the wild
                      garden of his.

                basketsful of nettle
                armsful of fennel

Magnolia's after-rain fragrance indecent almost,

we leave the garden for the woods—
        up Moss Creek we cross,
feet finding rocks.

Old homesite on far bank.

Places where people once slept, bricks,

impressions on the earth
        don't call them ruins.

There was a man. There was
            a woman & I have slipped to past tense.

    There was a wilderness I crossed

                & I am still crossing
                out words.
Neon beacon

of a yellow lady slipper orchid— its
scrotumlike pouch.

Crouching,   I touch the fleshy protuberance.

3

Chrysalis is a mess. All these beginnings

       of wings not fluttering in my chest.

A Luna moth on the glass

       clings.

We admire its color:

       pistachio ice cream. My dress

looks drab. It's late,

       he says, moth flinging its body

against glass. Why. Why.

       Why. A Luna emerges with no mouth,

only to mate then die. I don't tell him this.

       I am not empty,

I am open. Flinging myself
       against.

Against why.

       Against leaving.

My own body—

       its casing.

4

Out of a long untold season

I have come.
                        Cattails' seedfluff drifts over the pond
                        & already there is
                                    locust, wisteria, columbine, &
roses
groping
fences.

An old woman in cotton nightgown out
        sweeping the sidewalk, bare feet.

        Yes sad here like in everyplace
                even though yellow discs of coreopsis.

How crammedfull it is with people,
cats, houses, rain, slugtrails, chickens,
chainlink, oblivion, cigarettes, laughter,
alleyways, mosquitoes.

        How sweet, how

rotten. How I never want to leave
        or stay.

How I keep moving, restless.

Daylilies in the alley at dusk,
        wild peas, milk-vetch, mallow.
Sweet cherries, I spit out the pits.
        A rabbit, dead, its beaded eyes of fear,
fur matted. A piñata
        soggy: cavity of body
busted open: guts, spilled candy,
                        ants.

I trace the moon through   the traceless sky.

It strains me murkless
preens as if an egret,
curved white wing.

The Hours

1

Words in the mouth   gaps in the fences.
The ticking of days.

Earth uninhabited.   I am too grown feral
& acreages for sale.

The song of a cricket   rises over the long curves
of summer fields. The earth it parabolaes,

apexes at   alone intervals.
A sharp-shinned hawk screams.

June berries—   raspberries, blue,
wineberries, black, & peaches, bruised.

A fecund anxiety,
I make a pie   to quell it,
swim as the moon rises above the lake.

I float against the sky, rub against watery

frictions.

Not empty   but open.
Untouched   by nothing.

2

      Blue hydrangeas   bloom outside a
woods cottage &
      the questions   burn countless.

False awakenings
      leave me   soft in the ankles,
uncoil   the springs of the mattress.

      We embrace
        in the not-sayings of green,

books of poems opened to certain pages.

Stones clasp   to one another's surfaces
      or depths   through odd susurrations of the night.

You could say it isn't happening,
      that we are on the margins of once.

3

        Summer descends endlessly
        in the ovaries.   Queen Anne's lace

sways, umbel-headed, heavy.

      A dragonfly lays eggs
in the streambed touches its abdomen to wet
      stones. I take   amnesiac naps

in the groves of time.   I dream
      I am milk-full. A heron fishes
      in the shallows.

        I cannot have enough
        silence to speak of.

Between longest
daylight & night
my lips unkissed.

Voices   engines mimosa blossoms   & gasoline.
Cicadas pulse in the trees. Congregate,

exit nymphal exoskeletons.   Translucent shells
clouded eyes   stepped out of into wings

        into metallic   blue-green bodies—
        a mating   frenzy in the branches, the music.

            To deafen me to the noise of
            vacant
            spacethrum.

Later I walk across the ridge.   Amniotic streams
of moonlight in the   eyes, a whippoorwill
clear-throated singing.

4

The torque of the sky
in my hands.
I disappear into days of Joe-Pye weed

grown tall on the islands of the creek.

Horserush, reeds. Ferns sporulating.

I disappear. Viburnum's veiny
leaves. Miterwort, spleenwort, elderflower,
trillium. The names bring them nearer.

Field

1

The moon's a silver blade.
        I slice chanterelle mushrooms

like soft apricots, cool flesh in the palms.   Flesh when left
                alone digests debris   grows from rotting
    things.
Moist or clam-like I am hungry.
             As if the flesh
   were the only knowing, which it is

& what would the flesh contain   but seeds or pit or a silence
that crept under it.   Gills like miniscule cuts.

I took a road because   something caved in on me.
    On the   highway
passing fields   I keep going. Keep driving   clear
     out of myself   or the city. A deer—

its neck snapped cleanly.   Was thrown against the force
of its elated body   bounding across space   spine arced
    its lacerated chest pale honey.

    A voice
not lost but thrown across   what valleys of me,
     escaped what boundaries.   Leapt over what fences
   of he did not touch me.

I was walking. A buzz
in my head where he was
not.

Fields cleared   where once   there were trees.
Stalks of corn   like lightning struck   in the heat

bolts of cloth-like   husk,   a doll's dress you made as a child

& I am restless in my skin again.
        Strands spool out from the not-yet
        kernels, spilling beyond the
        husk prison.

        A grain of pollen   slides downward
              through the silk
                          into the ear.

2

Listen: a rustling.

An egret in the shallows where limbshadows

hang.

The lines of shore, water, roots exposed

exposing my winglessness.

I look through the trees: white porcelain body,
long neck & wing,
            an eye that pierces the surface.

A gloam spreads in the east—
            the fire that night is,
a burn in my head.

Where, egret,

do you dissolve in the water?

Into what versed layer?

Easing in   I slip under.

We emerge from baptisms

            cleansed

or gasping.

3

The moon two halves   of a mollusk.

A full globule   pearled in my nacre throat

to say something.

    At Big Creek we walk on the wall of the dam
    behind which water presses.

A man backflips off   plunges changes languages.

A cedar rots on the bluff above the river.   Rich musk
of its ceased xylem   interior striations engrained with fallen

beginnings fallen years   Dendritic cobwebbing grown thick

    it was everything   I needed.   Rain in

the morning   Halved from dreams in this

skin of measureless   thirsts.

Remembering the brine of our tongues.
    The opulent fires   & imprints of lost things
Records expunged & how we flood

them.   Erasures of water & what is shored up.

        What else to do but wipe clean
    the lens

    of our attention:

    look, a hibiscus
    opening.

4

Meniscus in the predawn dusk. I do not wake into its brief low arc from the cask
of sleep but glimpse through gauze of curtains the yellow glow. I dream the warm
dreams of snakes, muskrats curled into themselves. In the caves at Lascaux:
pollen grains of grasses excavated: to mean they bedded underneath
their ochre shadows near coals of rivercane torches or ashes. Like aurochs
we met in the dim light, eyes unglued. Musculature
of neck in darkness, trunk as if bison charcoaled & the musky hide-scents
or hunted, we—

The moon
slid on the track of its orbit & I was alone again with my unshackledness.

Light rests

below the earth—reaches up,

uncoils.

Screen creaks as I open it,
slams shut. Rattles on its hinges.

Flutter, rouse. A slow flush from thickets. I comb the edges of the field:
indigo

buntings, the blue elastic sheen of feathers.

Chicory

1

Moon: from proto-Germanic *menon*, "to measure"—

not in straight lines
      but circles, orbits, arcs.   It circles

    not the same way   twice.   Time becomes

more real & I am grown old again in August.

      The hay is dried baled twined
piled into gray barns whose walls lean
      at the edges of fields.
Bales round, spun like thread
      onto spools. Stalks of grass gold.
The stamp of your index occurs just once
      in the universe: as if inked, scribed—
I mean the eyes in the boards of barn's
      siding.
          I looked through the slats at
            bales radiant. Shafts of dusted   light
               caught   in rafters, beams.

If we could stall the sun. Scuffed the dirt with my heel.

This country unceasing. Unpaused in. My feet not leathered on the hard
earth as in childhood.   I mean there used to be love here, milkweed
seeds floating.   A pod burst open, hollowed.   The hallowed ground
      around fenceposts   where it grew.

Grainstalks sent up look like
      the world is full of days & unfamined.
The eyes are cisterns or silos storing angles of light, gathering

                  hours. A season
burnt.   Burrs not carried   on the hem of my pants. Hearts

         grown calloused
         & the skirts
         not lifted, fence-rails
         not climbed, straddled, horses
                              not saddled.

2

Jewelweed on the banks. Glowworms

blink in the interstices of weeds. He called

them foxfire as if it were another

world entirely   that tangled us, the moon

a pistil of nectar.   I keep starting over

from nothing.

Eyes submerged in the world

are made beautiful or a mystic

by what scours them—mica, schist,

a grain of sand. How I try to fix

the shapes of things against shape-

lessness. Ink them against blankness

or gone.

The nameless mollusks. Thick-skinned muscadines
slick inside.   Tart red berries of autumn olive, mottled.

Waspnests in windowsills, yellow jackets

at the panes. The webs of spiders

never swept between the legs of chairs.

3

I keep starting over again   like a thirst
            strikes   or the clutch went out
        & a chord & stutter   in the parking lot.

I mean this country of silences.   The stammers &
            these repetitions.   The moon's a silver fuse   that
                        drives us.

Mosquitoes   whine in the ears, a tone that
deafens.   The light is sapsucked

& I drain the dregs
of rosemary nettle mead
dredge the river
drink the honey fermented
as if the last drop.

4

Peaches picked too early like sunsets not yet
blushing the sky

sweeten in a paper bag,   then break against the teeth.

The blue of chicory on the roadsides.

A praying mantis at my doorstep
        like a priest administers a blessing &

I remember fingers   interlacing
            between intervals of gearshifting.

Yes neglected is growing
            & unvacant of the fuse that sparks it   —the tall grasses
                                                    nearing summer's end.

        What goes to seed
& scatters.

        The all-day percussives
of katydids like rapture.

Harvest

1

Earth on its spindle
         slips   as if   skipped a beat.

      A vinyl record: space
                              as high lonesome &
                              monarch migrations.
Time is due to gravity,
        magnets, or fields of buckwheat &
        orchards & the vocal cords.

     The seconds tick   & a fire
         burns in all the apple cores.

     How the eyes spin gold from dust
     of floors & dirt in crevices,

alight on the moth-littered
sills. Like there is anything

     but residue, sawdust, mildewed
     shower curtains. We've spun round before,

are threaded
to the past, spider-webbed. The beercans I once

     two-stepped through, long
     ago the cigarette stubs
how I think of.

        A snakeskin draped across hibiscus branches
        & what if we could shed us

find something new in the known skin,

beneath it.

> The hairpin curves around which I slid
> or scales ascended electric & rusted in the
> chest.   If my breasts were a milk & harvest.

2

Oyster mushrooms   & the accumulated recollections of piecrusts.
                    I measure rations of moon.

Grasshoppers senesce, a garden of grasses gone to seed   inscrutable
& fescued   how I am seed-heavy & headached & the root-tousled
earth   turns on me.

A house settles. I sweep spiders, the thresholds of in
& out dissolving & I déjà-vu.
      Fall again, recall the livewires that   our lips were, the smell
of his coffee.

Busted windowscreen.   Loose   gaskets & an oil pan gouged
on the gravel driveway.   I was snagged by the thorns
      of blackberry bushes   where I trespassed
           & a cow lowed mournful at dusk.

3

Be wilder.   Be more   quiet, earth-stunned
                      & unalone   in a house of ticking closets.

            The tiny pulses of crickets   like the pumping
of my blood.

I listen   as if at the other side of.

            A motor throttles & the faint throstle   of thrushes
              in the witch hazel outside the window.   Wrens,
                   nuthatches in the spinney.

      Gurgle of creek moaning
        vultures coo death in their roosts, toilet
runs, a ceramic trickle. The hound sleeps
       toenails clicking as he
                bounds in a dream.

How I try to fix

the sounds
of these

against
silence.

A gunshot's report

echoes over the nameless hills

        & the stillness

        that follows—

4

I fold inward   & go to the river.

Gravelly,   I idle   at the ragged nettle
                              & skunk cabbage.

Fleabane, *solidago*,
& fading sedges.   Spent bullet-shells,
hollow.

        Mists rise over the ridges.

Vines stray &
the world is very old.

                    Leaves yellowed:

        tulip poplar
        hickory
        walnut
        oak.

I say the names as if hallowing—
        to burnish this deciduous ness
against the page's blanknesses.

                Acorns scattered,   horse chestnuts.
                                Glean the fields. Harvest

tomatoes, corn, squash.   Persimmons clandestine in the
        branches, hazelnuts.

What to say but nothing

& gathering.
            The galaxy was night-
        spun I mean it was milk & a star

29

                    shot across it & burned to nothing
                                 or where did it go.

In the springhouse
crates of potatoes
cool in the dark &
cavernous must.

Fire

1

Dusk slips   away   & into the trees.
A plough's   rusted discs   bloom   with dawn.

What is sacred   or slips   through the
T e e t h :   the prayers,   recitations
    whispered

       as if I am   a repository   or   altar

the stoked embers   of my eyes,   still-
    heliotroping   sunflowers.   A hawk
 swoops.   It was always   salvific,
   even   celebratory,

even when   I was   tongue- tied.

In the burnt copses   I walk.
Watch from the ridges   the slow
flames of hills   spreading,
trace the lines   of old roadbeds &
I swear everywhere   there is a pale fire.

    A hum   in the earth   to the core   of it.

2

The ordinary humdrum of our footsteps
on the duff.
Together we went   & lost
            our way through beauty   & brokedownness
                        Footloose as if unfettered.
How to fritter time or save it.   Leaflitter layer,
my blown hair   sifts   into humus.   The earth
   is full of soil, specks of mica,   silvery,
   quartz,   crystalline,   trestle-crossed & transected.

Photographic oak leaf on the pond.   A memory-film
                                                    flickers
                                                    at the edges.

The pleasure   of fields in stillness,   deep grasses,
chafes of wheat or what weeds.   Keep looking
as if my eyes   had not already seen
                        thirty-three autumns.

Sorbus americanus   the mountain ash's
                        red berries—everything a torch or fuel
                        that bleeds me.

Trametes versicolor

                        the exuberant or   solemn tails of turkeys
                        flock fungally   across fallen trunks.

The woodpile's interlocking logs
show the sharp   lines of the axe: diamonds,
hexes.   How many   trees & liturgies fell to earth
at odd angles.

Deer float   through the trees in flares diaphanous,
streams of fur   ·   over fencewires.   Ears pricked
the intelligent posture   like whispers, eye-black
                        darts.

Deadfall, blowdown   like tapes unwound
or rewinded.   Pressed the windfall cider,
          swilled it.

The moon is distilled.   Sacred do not say
          but feel
this ground of stone & rock.
I mean it's too solid sometimes.

3

The pall & arousal of a rain that will not lessen.

      Drum of gutters, heartbeat. Noise

of what & cold snap. Or what not. Spine

      popping.

When each breath is a moment not

      empty & how we listen.

Back Creek: pools cascade, the stones

      sing I mean always hearing things.

He casts. Slack & the waiting,

      the invisible arc of line.

A speckled rainbow flutters
      spectral in his palm. Its slick of scales glint
again into the current.

      A blaze spread away from me—

the terse tongue & the feckless
                spells
    held
    under it.

Beyond the seeping treeline

the lantern of sunset.

4

Time's slow spinneret   spills

an architecture of ink.

Dew-shimmering threads   hang between tall
grass stalks in   the moonless morning.

The patterns of   fickle aeons   leave us
        rapt.

Kindling   broken,   meted,
in   lengths in   basket.

The Hunt

1

I weave through the deer-threaded woods   a weft circulatory,
    lymphatic. Language   loses me. I am abandoned   to the land.

The orphaned senses—
a scent, estrus left.

Buck rub   on roughened bark, the soft tufts.
Faint paths   tramped,   whispers of ligature.

Impressions of   heart-shaped hooves
            like well-trodden utterances.

The sodden calligraphy   of ungulates
    turns the hills to scrawl.

Presences   are fleet
    & yet   we are   so   marked by them.

A trail—
    ridge unscrolls under feet

the blood   both quick & slow at once.
This failure,   speech.

2

Lines of ice lace outward from corners in intricate
patterns on panes of glass.

The three-studded belt of Orion in the east.
The stars' cold gleam the proof of my breathing.

3

     Frozen ground
      ribbons of frost
like candy, smears
of crimson
     on the rime

slight swing
on the hook
     blood draining
     how long
with no one
to see

     a private undoing
     as if to lessen
the hands'
killing

     skinned &
     quartered

bucket of
scraps
     to the dog
     like
     redemption

          the sudden
          green of
          spruces

     the stars
     rearranging

4

Iron in the pipes.   Percolator on the woodstove & the day
broke.   Venison in corn tortillas.

I gather wild oregano   on the hillslope's cherty terraces.
Here is mullein. Barberry, its bare   & thorny branches.
The rattle of milkweed pods.   The fields gone ochre-umber.

November's   sudden
stillness sudden brown   stillness.

Evergreen

1

I never knew the spruce
though it weighted & shadowed
my sleep   & I woke to it each morning
          through the window
                    I have only just seen
its fallen boughs beneath in the dead grass   like eels writhing
                    No, I have not seen   the
          spruce
how sorrowful, eccentric its limbs
          look draped   with the dyed pelts of sheep

     There   is the cellar
          in the hillside— its stones slick with new rain
                    a steel wheel   leaned against it

Ivy clings to cracks   A cellarfull
          of visionless potatoes   sleeping   tuberously in
crates—

                    I have not seen any of this

          How the spruce towers above
          the woodshed
                    the kindling stacked on pallets in the dim,
                    a side-lying gas can, chainsaw lubricant,
                    the chopping block outside

     Wood's spheres, rings, spectrums split—   bands streak the wedges like
                              long-exposure stars

          I didn't notice   the spruce's pruned lower limbs
                    protruding like pegs,   the lowest prune-scars
          like eyes clouded over

        gazing coniferous   at my pacings in the kitchen

   Looking up, the limbs   are runes
                      cast across   a white canvas
         The spruce's sap coagulates, runs

Now I see it   yes   a resurrected mammoth
         an extinct god   *Picea rubens*

Ravens   circle overhead
          scanning the endless haze of the earth

2

Here   the hollow sings.

       The creek's rickety trickle
            an aqueous trill through stones.

I haven't been alone   to hear it.

             He stands bent at the waist

             head hanging over the bank &

             I wash his winter-pilgrim head.

Fill   a pot with the shock of cold
clear water,   pour it over.

It runs
       through his hair
along backs of ears,
       lobes, on a path
to his pious clavicle.

I see the calm   flinches in his brow.

                The finches have stayed the winter.

       The stream racket incandescent
in the mercurial morning,

           a rush of white behind the eyes.

Bulbs below ground
take careful measurements.

       Stones slip into the folds of stream's
curtains, disappear—

another layer of sound somewhere
in the halls of the air.

3

A holt of hemlocks: the sacrosanct dark in them.

A barred owl's neck-craned stare locked to mine:

tried to hold the gaze

  —it lifted, swooped, glided,
  swift—

like I never saw it.

4

I make these marks as if   who knows when

I will   see again

beyond the ceaseless trespasses   of pasts & futures
that serrate   my concept   of his ribs & shoulders.

He was a forest decomposing.   The lichen
spread across his chest,   moss covered his mouth
          & I could not quit
          seeing moon shards in the pines.

                    Tire-tracks: wheels mudspun, the tread—
                                        to remember   even this.

                              Hepatica's waxed lobes, pipsissewa,
                              the ash-green leaves of rhododendron
                              like ashes scatter

                              above the stream you haven't seen.

What stays? Savor it.   Love will leave
          you lean   leave you   brackish.

Hide the meat   between your cheek & teeth.

                    Make wreaths of evergreen, running cedar,
                                        galax. Watch the juncos
fatten. Watch them

thresh the seed

grind you to clear witness

knead you to pliant

or quit life's fires.

46

Ash

1

Subtle   humble   country flames
A strange warp to the   shapes   of   things

        Dürer's rabbit   on haunches
                in a frame on the wall, its motley textures
of fur   the animal body drawing
        heat into its core.

The river   frozen now in its flow.

                A wildish ink   loops & curves—

track me line to line

        for miles

        The storms of atoms
        he stilled in me
        how he

                An apparition—   smoke from chimney
                        plays across the snow, dances billowy

        shadows, a cumulus of gloom against

    expanse of bright blanket,

            night's shank.

Electric current sings quiet in the power lines.

2

The claustral rhododendrons. The dank cavern of the hollow. Moon when the deer shed their antlers. I sit on a rock where the basswood's roots twist. Watch creep of cinereous water under ice, locked in darkness, how it captures turbulence.

        Down
   drive down
      to the bone-quick

cinder sky, occipital shock

   of the eyes expanding

into winter's unquitting

   galaxy,

   lines of the forked tines.

O, dusk closes,   a pang in the chest. A clanging.   Moonlight strafes onto the ice,

lights the shards   the way glass shatters.

3

A deer's corpse   blossoms
                                  from the river's shoals

Ballooning, acrid
                         Unfading pigments
                         of blood

Days pass
                              vultures gut the carcass strip it of
                              intestines, muscle, heart

I stare into the rib-dark
                              crescent of its chest

     Where its lungs once were,

          riffles moving through

4

    Curious visions strike
upon the eyes

    become verses
for my vast litany

    of what will not last,
can't.

Memory seeks
    to transcend

the transience of things.
    Ars longa; vita brevis—

page as preservation
    method.

Venus sears in the cast-iron night.

Marrow

1

        If the hills seem razed

if the moon seems poor

        if the fields seem bare

if the riverbed seems tired

           blame the earth its wild tilt.

Thank the stars when you see

         slow cows, a light   snowfall

dusting their backs.

2

The littered road, friendless

    town.

If I thought these words

    were worth   even the worry

of the inkscrawls,   worth my salt,

    I would set   my teeth to gnashing

more often against   the gray sky

& its   snow squalls.

If I thought   my words could call forth

    life's riches   spin the light to gold
      paint the hills' browns timeless

    I would whisper them into
  your eyes.

3

Then after a night of his breathing I lie awake listening as if to store it in the
cells a bee fretting the honey of memory's hive in the kitchen he turns me
window-facing hands on shoulders toward the snowdrops that have
bloomed while we slept white bells hanging from green stems the full-
mouthed vowels of O & O & we are full of one another's mouths

        Later I disappeared into the walls, the snowdrops
        hollowing out my ribs   fierce with memory,
the threat of forget ting

In dreams there are   basements   that greet me
      with the cool force of their darkness,   passages below
                    where we keep residence

        That day
          after he left   a sky opaque as cataracts

   a longing mean as knives

4

There are shady patches of ground
      where the snow remains long after
the rest is melted,   all the shadow-kept
      pockets calling light to them for once.

          So let   the earth swallow us—
the press of my feet to the muck of it,   god
               is in here

        in the veins, blood, semen, mud,
               late winter's boil.

    Let the moon pity us.

Let it gape
& mock
& gawk

& it ripped   out my tongue in the twilight.

Yes   I said   is   in the melt, marrow, burn
              is   in the fire in my fingers.

          Purple crocuses
             push up the soil.
          Yellow daffodils
             nod.
          Trout lilies
             open on Cove Mountain.

Erythronium umbilicatum
      cool mottled leaves livery &
          shy flowerheads turned
    to the dirt.

How can the world call itself lonely

when mountains go inward & open like this?

      Born   of the bone of the moon.

Sap

1

Then there are nights of freeze, torrents

    of lacework stars I forgot

Then days when the sap rises

    through the hearts of trees

from roots' sweetness

    into the crowns

I lay on the earth the way

    fires sleep in the woodpile

2

One must have a mind   of sap

                              & he tapped
the trees
                drill & spile   sapwater
                drip dripping   in ping-plinks   in buckets

      I spired

                into the maple crowns.

No mind knows   really how sap flows

ascends past gravity toward buds, branches—

                        it's xylem's secret. It isn't the mind

                            but the body

                    that must keep it

or one must have a tongue to taste it.

                  His eyes   went jasper.

                  We boiled   the liquid.

Last cold snapped us   down deep

            to the knees   killed the irises.

Earth grew hushed   as if spurned

     by spring   & he lay down among me.

3

There are foals in the rag-tag pastures
                    calves on shaky knees donkeys on
spindly shins flocks of wild turkeys
The weeping cherry is flowering
        & everything happens too fast
Its petals fall like confetti from a party
        that's already over, just as it begins

& let everything happen.   Mustard-yellow
        fields & grieve everything.
Sorrow is wild. Sorrow is true.   Sorrow
        is roots. Sorrow is our   richest   blood.

                    Rue anemone speckles the bare forest
        floor.

                    Above in a thin blue sky

                    the day-moon's bone bloom.

4

Green slips through
the eye of the needle
faster
        than   a man can   walk into heaven,

stitches the heart's rough   edges, quilts
        each square   & quadrant. The ground quakes
with one green   rupture after another.

I never wanted   so much   as squadrons of geese
        overhead in vees   & plantain-leaved pussytoes'
        tight-packed bouquets,   skunk cabbage's

surreal infestations of   stink, starlike clusters
        of bluets   the bluebird's wings, red buds' smears
                        against the blue of mountains on the horizon.

A duck's iridescent green
                        feathers, just the subtlest of
gestures.   Bees hovering at violet, crabapple,

zooming flower to flower, columbine flaring
        over the serpentine water,   spiders   weaving orbs

                in the silken halls of the air—

I never wanted so much   as doing nothing more than seeing

                        thread & thread

                                & thread & breathing.

Flight

1

Become devotee
        spew testament

to this milk-green sorcery
        a rural conjury of color.

All that grows,
        germinates, slaked
& awaked in me a thirst
        for salvation & ferment

I wanted nothing so much
        as phlox's spread & pink

the river's pockets of still
        to swallow me whole   & florid

or him to ascend grass-
        high at the waist

I sought it
        Seekingly
            I walked

bent to
        trillium triumphant & large-leafed

pastel-petaled
        I wanted   nothing
so much   as

2

Wood ducks spooked
    from gentle currents
        lift up quacking, necks straight
           as arrows, pointing
        upriver like flint
           toward a target.

        What the soul
           leaves unasked
    the ducks' flight
        answers.

3

A cool sandstone wind, the light dissolves
The night is traceless a coal train hisses
into the lonesomest of places along the tracks
Between us sing starless silver rivers

4

A skunk's prints on the bank,   mink's.

The wood thrush flutelike. A tender fog

      lifts from the surface. The dogwood's

      milkglass petals bright the gaps in the under-

story, more lush by increments measure-

less & less gaps & bursting more.   For example the

      wood sorrel galore & idolatrous, azalea

      a resolute perfume. Scattered renditions

of golden ragwort, the green's wide dominion—

a carpet of moss, of stonecrop, unfurling

      ferns, fungi pushing forth. Goldfinches'

      heavy bobbing yellow bodies ground-flirting,

grass-skirting at growthy edges where the green

begins & does not beg pardon from the dust

              & does not end.

Ephemeral

1

Let it not end.   Let it   spread, our kin-dom come & never amen
in every notch, crevice, crack, fissure, interstice.
In every place a seed or spore is sown with no sparing wind,
takes hold. The fringe tree serried of honeyed
blossoms richly charged. Bleeding heart flush.
Saxifrage, geranium, buttercup besets each foot's press
to the surfeit-swollen land. Eyes feast on the fat of the soil
& hands full tendril toward stems of fire-pink, spring-beauty.
New vowels form, the breath rises up from consonant-constant
earth. A spirit rises from the things & into us & ours join
in the saying over it of the names like hymns, like blessings or
baptisms. In unison said what was writ & almost before they could
be said rose & returned again to dust before us: bellwort,
bluebells, cutleaf toothwort, yellowroot— short-lived but passed
through life's leafy language long enough. Like prayers smoke-sent
we spoke them on the Maury River & elsewhere, all over—

2

The days lengthen like velvet.

Moths thicken the moonless night
            heave   themselves at windowscreens   toward

     the glowing rooms   of the house.

Designs of desire   seeking fire,   wick's
    blaze.

    They circle, veer,
dive—   a timbre of wings & sizzle.

   Have faith   though the flames
                    consume us.

Love is not born   once   but must

   give birth   to itself again & again.

A cocoon moon emerges from clouds.

               Moths

               combust

               through the atmosphere & fall as

        dust

3

    Peonies lucid as white seas

beneath the sun, the

        day's speechless charms.

        What's to come of all days'

drained sweetnesses? Ants crawl,

        drink the unknown nectars.

4

& it will end &
everything bears us
on wings of attention

though we've been here,
will be again, the moon emaciated

A water thrush flits
among the underbrush

bluebird flashes
in the hemlock's branches

red-winged blackbird sails
from locust to fence

wood thrush vaults
to the canopy,

a wing-filled chantry

Feathers incense the ceiling
of the sanctorum forest

the scarlet tanager a doctrinal flame
in the throat of our saying
a blaze in the heart of our knowing

A mourning dove at the pulpit:
a sermon on how to love.

I lash my heart's weight
to its gray pinions. It carries
it on a calm dirgelike song

Listen, a towhee returns, melodious

Listen, made manifest are manifold

throats & wings

that return to us   return us

to love's lilt,
fierce flight

that sings us blessed—

Acknowledgments

Offerings of wineberries and rhododendron blossoms to my fifth-great-grandparents Margaret Weaver and William Morricle, who are buried facing the east on the West Fork of the Little River in Floyd, Virginia, on the land adjacent to where I wrote most of these poems. I thank the ancestors for calling me back to the house of the rising sun and rising moon, before I knew who they were or why I was there. I thank the land of the abundant dawn. And offerings of muscadines & chicory flowers to the ancestors of the French Broad River Valley, Holston River Valley, and Tennessee Valley, their knowledge and love of the land. I am in deep and humble gratitude to the Yesan (Tutelo) people, who cared for the land of the abundant dawn for untold generations, and to the Tsalagi (Cherokee), who cultivated the soil that formed my bones. A portion of the proceeds from this book will be donated to the #LandBack movement.

I raise my goblet of moonlight to those who listened to or read parts of this manuscript along the way, for your interest and encouragement: Janisse Ray, Rose McLarney, Thorpe Moeckel, Robert Moor, Alan Bajandas, Adam Welz, Christopher Shaw, Bill McKibben, Scott Honeycutt, and Andrew Zawacki. For your friendship during a difficult time, a warm hug to Shelly Fox, Melanie Huber, and Sarah McCarthy. May Luna moths flutter your way. I am grateful to Marc Jolley and the team at Mercer for bringing this book into the world.

And thank you to the moon: keeper of our time, teacher of cycles both constant and changing; moon, our meter, master of the rhythms of life and origin of poetry. "The first most obvious regularly repeating refrain in our ancestors' lives, the light that bestowed the gift of regular increments came from the moon," as Joshua Schrei has said in his ode to the moon. "What a gift, to have something that is both constant and that pulses between disappearance and reappearance." Moon, ending and beginning again and again. What a gift. I am ever in awe and gratitude. May the whippoorwill always sing for you.